MW00823924

STORY OF THE MORNING STAR,

The Children's Missionary Vessel.

BY

REV. HIRAM BINGHAM, Jr.,

MISSIONARY TO MICRONESIA.

BOSTON:
PUBLISHED BY THE AMERICAN BOARD.

Missionary House, 33 Pemberton Square.

1866.

BV 2.671
E.

RIVERSIDE, CAMBRIDGE:
STEREOTYPED AND PRINTED BY
H. O. HOUGHTON AND COMPANY

TO THOSE WHO BUILT THE FIRST MORNING STAR,

AND

TO THOSE WHO WISH TO BUILD ANOTHER.

—◆—

* MY DEAR YOUNG FRIENDS, — You have all heard of the missionary vessel that was sent to the Pacific Ocean in 1856; not a few of you took stock in her. Perhaps you have read about her in the " Missionary Herald," the " Journal of Missions," the " Youth's Dayspring," the " Friend," or in a book written by Mrs. Warren. Well, the little craft has been sold. She was almost worn out; and it was thought better to build a new vessel than to repair the old one.

As I was the first missionary that went to sea in her, and have known her ever since, the Secretaries of the American Board a few weeks ago requested me to write a short story about her, in order that you may see how much good she has done, and so be all the more glad to aid in building another *Morning Star* to take her place.

From the shortness of the time allowed me, to say nothing of my imperfect health, I should have been unequal to the task, had I not received much assistance from others. A great deal of this I have had from one who has known the *Morning Star* as long as I have, and has been my companion in nearly all my voyagings in her; and I take pleasure also in saying that kind friends at the Missionary House have, by their valued suggestions and criticisms, and in other ways, added not a little to the interest which this " Story of the Morning Star " may be thought to possess. Such as it is I offer it to you. And my prayer is that it may lead you to pity the heathen more deeply than ever. May I not hope that you will think more of that love, so great, so free, which has made it possible for them, as well as for you and me, to see the Lord Jesus in his Heavenly kingdom !

H. B., JR.

Missionary House, May 19th, 1866.

EXPLANATORY NOTE.

THOSE who desire to pronounce the native words found in the following pages as they are pronounced in the Pacific, will please to remember that

a is generally like a in father.
e is   "   "   a in late.
i is   "   "   i in ravine.
o is   "   "   o in note.
u is   "   "   oo in pool.
ai is "   "   i in fine.
au is "   "   ow in now.
n is   "   "   ng in sing.

As the names of certain islands will occur very frequently, I will add that,

Ponape is to be pronounced nearly as if written Po'-nah-pa.*
Kusaie   "   "   Koo-sy'-a.*
Ebon   "   "   A-bóne.
Apaiang   "   "   Ap-py-áhng.
Tarawa   "   "   Tar'-rah-wah.

Please to notice the marks which show where the *accent* is to be placed.

* The final a in these two words, as also A in A-bone, has the sound of a in late.

CONTENTS.

vi CONTENTS.

CHAPTER XII.

ILLUSTRATIONS.

STORY OF THE MORNING STAR.

CHAPTER I.

THE LANDS SHE WAS TO VISIT.

WHEN Balboa, in 1513, first looked upon the mighty
Pacific from a mountain-top on the Isthmus of Panama,
and called it the South Sea, how little did he know
of the thousands of islands which studded its placid
bosom, stretching ten thousand miles towards the setting
sun ! No Captain Cook, or Marshall, or Gilbert, or any
one else, had described them, or even seen them. Now,
however, enough could be told about them to fill many
large books.

On one of them I was born; and as you speak of
America as *your* native land, so I sometimes speak of
the Pacific as *my* birthplace and childhood-home.
There too was the field of my labors as a missionary,
and there the *Morning Star* has been going about on
her errands of love.

The Pacific is so large that people who make geog-
raphies have divided it into several portions. One
they call Polynesia, which means "many islands;"
and another they call Micronesia, which means "little
islands." In both divisions we find some high islands;
but many are mere coral reefs. The Ladrone and some
of the Caroline Islands are high; but the Gilbert and
Marshall Islands are all low. One· of the missionaries
has beautifully described this island world, by saying,

"The whole is studded with ocean gems, as if the
mirror of the starry sky above it."

Come with me, while I take you to those parts of
the Pacific which your little vessel has visited. We
will start from New York, in a steamer, for Aspinwall
on the Isthmus of Panama. This we can reach in
eight days; and there we will take the cars across the
Isthmus, passing not far from the mountain where Balboa first saw the Pacific. By steamer we shall reach
San Francisco in thirteen days. Thence we will go
in a sailing vessel toward the southwest. With a
good wind, we shall have sailed more than twenty-five
hundred miles in ten or twelve days, and shall have
reached the high, volcanic island of Hawaii.

Now let us imagine that from the top of Mauna
Kea, (nearly three miles high,) which I once tried to
reach, but did not, we are looking off far toward the
south. If the world was flat, and we had eyes sharp
enough, we should see the Marquesas Islands, about two
thousand miles distant, — high, rugged, volcanic. Looking off toward the southwest, we should see the Micronesian Islands, the nearest of which are more than
two thousand miles away, and the farthest more than
four thousand.

Let us dwell upon this beautiful sight. Some of
these islands, you see, are clustered together in groups;
while some may be called "lone isles of the sea."
Some of them are volcanic; and by this we mean that
they have been made by the lava which is thrown up
by volcanoes in the sea. These are generally covered
with forests; and on them you would find, if you could
go there, lovely valleys, babbling brooks, birds of bright
plumage and sweet song. You would also find trees
that yield figs, limes, oranges, bread-fruit, bananas, and
guavas. Pine-apples, melons, yams, and sweet potatoes, you would expect to see, of course, in great abun-
dance.

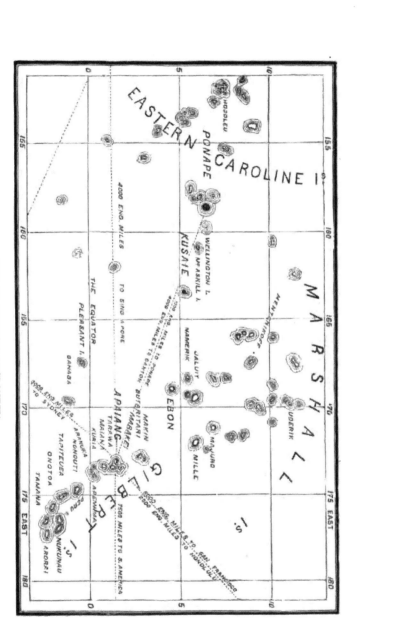

MAP OF EASTERN MICRONESIA.

The larger part of the islands of Micronesia are low coral islands; and they have all been built up by animals. These little creatures began their work, if such it may be called, on the side of some island, high, low, or submerged, not more than one hundred and twenty feet below the surface of the sea. And when the foundation upon which they were building, sunk slowly down into the deep water, (for all these islands are believed to have sunk,) the patient workers kept right on, striving to reach the surface, till at last they gained the victory. The dry land, if any, had disappeared; the fruit of their labor alone remained! What a monument to the industry and skill of these wonderful architects! Everywhere in Micronesia, therefore, you will find coral islands, most of them with a great lake or lagoon in the centre, so that you might call them "hollow islands."

These central lakes are generally connected with the ocean by one or more ship-channels. In the largest of these all the navies of the world might anchor with perfect safety. The rims of land which surround the lagoons are very narrow; so that you might run across them in three or four minutes. The soil is poor, and often very barren. There are no springs, no running streams, no hills; and there are but few land-birds and few flowers. Cattle, sheep, and goats can live there but a short time; but, strange to say, multitudes of human beings have their homes there. Alas, in what darkness!

> " The immense Pacific smiles,
> Round ten thousand little isles
> Haunts of violence and wiles."

CHAPTER II.

THE PEOPLE SHE WAS TO VISIT.

I HAVE told you of the regions to which the *Morning Star* was bound. It is time to speak of the people to whom she was going; for men are worth a great deal more than the lands in which they live.

You have all heard about the Sandwich Islanders, or Hawaiians, — how they cast away their idols, and how they became a Christian nation in less than thirty years after the first missionaries (of whom my father was one) went among them.

The Marquesas Islanders are much like the Hawaiians in looks and language; and before the latter received the Gospel their religion was much the same. In one respect, however, they were very different. Few of the latter were ever cannibals, while the former were universally so. Dr. Gulick places the Marquesans among the "more sprightly and intelligent of the Polynesian tribes." "Their free democracy from earliest days, fostered by their sequestered valleys," he says, "has been the great outer obstacle to the Gospel; but it has given them an independence, and a certain firmness of character, which renders them less impressible to foreign motives and influences, and has given a subsoil to cultivate, from which we may hope for growths of some permanence. We see this in those who have been converted. The mien and conversation of several of them is that of men convinced, and ready to stand by their convictions, even in the face of the scoffer from foreign lands."

The people of the different groups of Micronesia have

some things in common; but in other things they differ
greatly. They are much alike in color; they are somewhat alike in looks, in religion, in manners, and customs.
The Gilbert and Marshall Islanders are of the usual size;
the Strong's Islanders (Kusaieans) are rather smaller. Mr.
Damon says that the Marshall Islanders are "unmistak-
ably of Japanese extraction," and the Gilbert Islanders
"most strikingly like the Hawaiians."

If you would paint one of the Micronesians, you must
give him a dark skin, — here copper, there olive; you must
make his hair straight and black; you must make his eyes
black also; and you must be sure not to forget the "tattoo"
marks on his body, of which he is so very proud.

The people of one group cannot understand the language
of another; but the missionaries find that many words are
common to all the groups. It sometimes happens that the
men living on these islands are drifted away in their canoes
to a great distance; but they soon learn to converse in
any new tongue which they have occasion to use. You
know, of course, that before the missionaries visited them
they had no books; neither could they read or write, so
dark were their minds; but, alas, their hearts were darker
still!

The unconverted Micronesians are all liars. The fathers
lie, the mothers lie, and the children lie. Indeed, they
seem just as ready to deceive as to speak the truth. They
are much disposed to steal, moreover. They steal from
one another, from the ships which visit them, and frequently from missionaries who live among them. In their
way they are very covetous. They know very little about
nice houses, railroads, bank-stocks, fine horses, and fine
clothes; but they are greedy of fishhooks, tobacco, plane-
irons, large knives, scented oils, and beads. They often
treat their women with great cruelty, beating them, stab-
bing them, making slaves of them. The little children,
for the most part, have much kindness shown to them;
but I am sorry to say that they do not honor their fathers

and their mothers. And I will add that very little respect
is paid to old people. They generally treat strangers
kindly. offering food and drink to those who call on them.
None of the Micronesians are cannibals: but they are
very passionate and· revengeful. Hence they are much
given to fighting and killing one another. A great many
murders are committed every year.

The Micronesians can hardly be called *idolaters ;* that
is, they do not bow " down to wood and stone : " but they
are heathen nevertheless. and they worship false gods. I
think we might call them " spiritualists." They believe
there are *a great many* spirits which have to do with them.
They set up stones in honor of them. (see one of these
stones in the extreme left of the picture opposite page 16,)
and often make offerings of food to them: for they are
much afraid of them. Some persons profess to hold intercourse with these spirits. In the Gilbert Islands the
priests decide that a spirit is present. not by his *knocking,*
as some people in America do. but by his *whistling.*

They have many superstitions which it would take a
whole book to describe : but I have said enough to give
you some idea of the tribes which the *Morning Star*
was to visit. I have said enough to show you that the
Micronesians were poor heathen, needing the Bible to tell
them that Jesus had died to save them as well as us. You
see that such people could not be happy in heaven. The
blood that cleanseth from all sin. must be sprinkled upon
them before they can be admitted to that holy place.

CHAPTER III.

WHAT HAD BEEN DONE BEFORE HER VISIT.

I HAVE told you what kind of people the Micronesians were; and I have shown you how much they needed the Bible. Now let us see what Christians had done to give them the Gospel before the children sent the *Morning Star* to them. Of what had been done for the Marquesans I will speak in another place.

When the Hawaiians became a Christian people, not a few of them were willing to carry the Gospel to others who were ignorant of it, as they themselves had been; and the missionaries were glad to have them do this, in order that the churches to which they belonged might take a more active part in the salvation of the world, and receive a better training for all good works at home. They could not well go to China, or India, or Japan; for those countries were far off, and their languages were hard to learn. The islands of which we have been speaking were very small, it is true; but they were much nearer, and the people were more like themselves, in manners, and habits, and ways of living. To these, therefore, it was decided that some of them should be sent, and with them a few Americans, to cheer and counsel them, to translate the Scriptures, and to prepare books.

For this purpose three men, Mr. Snow, Dr. Gulick, Mr. Sturges, and their wives, sailed from the United States for Micronesia, the two former in 1851, and the latter early in 1852. They went first to the Sandwich Islands. While they were there, two Hawaiians, Kaaikaula and Opunui, with their wives, Debora and Doreka, were selected to accompany them to Micronesia.

But how should they get to their field of labor? There were no ships going back and forth between the Sandwich Islands and any of the groups of Micronesia. It seemed best, therefore, to buy a small schooner, which might take them there, and carry supplies to them afterwards. Her name was the *Caroline;* and in July, 1852, these five men and their wives set sail for their future home. Mr. Clark, one of the older missionaries at the Sandwich Islands,· and Kekela, pastor of a church on Oahu, went to help them in getting a foothold, after which they were to return again.

That you may know more about this Kekela, I will say that he was educated (as I was in part) by the kindness of a Boston merchant, once an officer of the brig *Thaddeus,* which took the first missionaries to the Sandwich Islands. He has been for many years, and is now, a missionary to the Marquesas Islands. Just before he sailed in the *Caroline,* he made a public address, which will give you some idea of the man. "I am a native of these islands," he said. " My parents were idolaters, and I was born in times of darkness. A short time ago all our people were heathen; they worshipped a great variety of gods; they were engaged in war; they were addicted to stealing and robbery. Man and wife did not live together and eat together, as now; they took no care of their children. . . . But a great light has arisen over us. . . . The Bible has driven away our darkness, overturned our heathenish customs, and caused a great improvement in our condition. Because the Word of God has been given us in our own language, we have learned to read; and all the people have learned to read it, old and young. It has been scattered all over the land, and taught all the people to do right. Therefore the people live peaceably; parents take some care of their children; the Sabbath is observed; the laws are regarded, and all dwell securely. . . . What, then, is more reasonable than that we Hawaiians should extend to other

nations in this ocean the blessings of the Gospel ? Those
tribes are now what we were a short time ago,—degraded,
wretched idolaters. Shall we not have pity on them, as
the people of God in the United States have had pity on
us ? "

The *Caroline* touched first at Butaritari, or Pitt's Island,
in the Gilbert group. On going ashore, the missionaries
visited the *maneaba*, (large council-house.) Learning that
there were just such buildings on other islands, they could
not help remarking to each other, — " Here are houses for
public Christian worship already erected, waiting for those
who shall proclaim the word of life." Not that the people had any such thought ; but God's ways are not as our
ways. How well they were adapted to such a use, you
will learn from the picture on the opposite page. You
have before you an immense roof, resting upon large
coral stones, some three feet from the ground, neatly
thatched with the pandanus leaf.

But though there were a great many people on this
island, as also on other islands of this group, the missionaries were not ready to leave any of their number
there. And so they passed on, some six hundred miles,
to Strong's Island, or, as the natives call it, Kusaie, a perfect " gem of the sea," of which I shall say more hereafter.
Here they decided to leave Mr. Snow and Opunui.

These brethren were very kindly received by the highest chief of the island, who was called King George. He
could speak a little English, and so could some of his
people. The missionaries were surprised at this, when
they remembered how seldom the Kusaieans had seen
either Americans or Englishmen.

Let me give you a specimen of King George's English.
He was telling the missionaries how he had forbidden the
making of intoxicating drinks ; and this is what he said :
" Plenty white men speak me, ' Very good, tap cocoa-nut-
tree ; get toddy.' Me say, ' No ; no good.' Plenty men
get drunk on shore ; too much row ; me like all quiet.

GILBERT ISLAND MAREABA.

No tap cocoa-nut-tree on Strong's Island.' " I am sure
you will say that King George was a wise ruler, even
though you may think his English somewhat rough and
jagged. And he deserves this testimony also, that he
was always kind to Mr. and Mrs. Snow and their companions. He had promised to be " all same father " to
them, and he kept his word. They were very sorry
when he died ; but they hoped that he was prepared for
the " better home." His dying charge to his son and the
other chiefs was, " Take good care of the missionaries."

After the visit of the *Caroline* to Strong's Island, she
went some three hundred miles farther west to Ascen-
sion Island, or, as the natives call it, Ponape. This is
one of the largest islands in Micronesia. It is high
and very fertile ; and the inhabitants at that time were
supposed to be about ten thousand. The missionaries
had been afraid that they might not be able to land ;
but the way was open, and Mr. Sturges, Dr. Gulick.
Kaaikaula, and their wives, commenced their work immediately on that dark shore.

In 1855 Mr. Doane and Kamakahiki, with their
wives, sailed from Honolulu in a whale-ship, to join
the mission on Ponape. The same year Dr. and Mrs.
Pierson, from the United States, reached Honolulu on
their way to Kusaie. They did not know when or
how they could get there from the Sandwich Islands;
but God had provided a way. The barque *Belle* was
soon to cruise near that island, and the captain kindly
consented to take them on board. Kanoa and his wife
Kaholo, both of them Hawaiians, went with them.

But I must tell you more of this barque *Belle* ; for
it was she that prepared the way for sending the Gospel to the low islands of Micronesia. She touched at
several of the Gilbert Islands ; and in this way Dr. Pierson and Kanoa were able to learn much about them.
They found that a great many people lived there,
although the soil would not produce garden vegetables ;

and Dr. Pierson thought that missionaries might live
there too. "They are the last persons," he said, "to
choose a field because it is easy." Both he and Mrs.
Pierson were willing, therefore, to return, and occupy
one of them in the name of the Lord Jesus.

The *Belle* next proceeded to the Marshall Islands;
and there Dr. Pierson became acquainted with a leading chief, called Kaibuke, and with his sister, Nemair.
No white men were then living in that group; and as
this chief had promised to take care of him, if he would
live there, he felt that it might be his duty to do so.
"To us," he said, "the field seems exceedingly inviting;
and we doubt not it will prove so to any one who may
be allowed the privilege of teaching this people the
way of life."

The *Belle* arrived at Kusaie on the 6th of October,
1855; and Dr. Pierson began to labor there, hoping,
nevertheless, to return to the Marshall Islanders at an
early day. Next April a fleet of canoes which had gone
adrift, with many of these very people on board, reached
Kusaie, and with them he became well acquainted.
After a few months, they set out for their homes, distant some three hundred miles; but Dr. Pierson did
not think it safe to go with them in their frail barks,
fastened together, not with iron, but with cocoa-nut
cord, and using mats for sails. He chose, rather, to
wait for a safer conveyance. Thus were the isles waiting for the law of the Lord, —

> —— "the powers of darkness yield,
> For the Cross is in the field,
> And the light of life revealed."

*

CHAPTER IV.

WHY SHE WAS NEEDED.

THE *Caroline*, which took out the first missionaries to Micronesia, was soon sold for lack of money to sail her. This was a sad blow to them; for they all felt that they needed a vessel of their own. Whale-ships, it is true, touched at their islands now and then; not so, however, as to be depended on. If you had been with them, you would have felt just as they did. Let me tell you why.

A missionary packet would bring them tidings from their *native land*. Mr. Snow's mother died, and it was two years before he heard of it! How, think you, could the missionaries have lived through our terrible war, if they had been obliged to wait two years for "the news"?

Such a vessel would supply them with proper *food*. They needed salt meat, flour, rice, sugar, and other articles which you have in your pleasant homes. Before the *Morning Star* was built, they suffered very much for the want of these things.

Such a vessel would give the *sick* the benefit of a sea-voyage. Before the children had built the *Morning Star*, Dr. Gulick wrote home from Ponape, concerning his wife, — "Her health is gradually failing. She much needs more exercise and relaxation than I can give her here. Were it possible, I should wish her to go to the Sandwich Islands for a time."

Such a vessel would be a *protection* to the missionaries. There are a great many bad men in the Pacific; and if they should get the idea that nobody cared for one

of these servants of Christ, they might rob him or kill
him. But the *Morning Star* has told them that thousands of good people, far away, are looking after his
welfare.

With such a vessel they could *preach Christ more
freely* to the Micronesians. They could go from island
to island, where no white man had ever been; so that
the first words from strange lips should be of "the great
salvation." Mr. Doane said, before the *Morning Star*
was sent to Micronesia, that he felt very much as if
he were in sight of a wrecked sailor on a huge rock,
around which the angry sea was dashing furiously,
utterly unable to reach him! He seemed to see the people beckoning to him to give them the Bible, and yet
he could not do it.

Let me show you just how the case stood in 1855.
The *Caroline*, in taking missionaries to Kusaie and
Ponape, had passed the Gilbert Islands on the left,
where there were some 30,000 or 40,000 heathen, and
the Marshall Islands on the right, where there were
at least 10,000. She touched, as we have seen, for a
few days at Butaritari, one of the most northerly of
the Gilbert Islands. The missionaries pitied these poor
heathen very much; and they hoped that the Gospel would some day be preached to them. Hawaiian
missionaries might easily be found who could live on
these coral rims; and we have seen that there were
American missionaries who would be glad to labor there.
What should be done? Should these Marshall and
Gilbert Islanders be left, as they had been for so many
ages, to live and die without hearing about their Saviour? If not, somebody must go and live among them.

It was decided to state the case to the children in
America, and to ask them to build a missionary vessel.
The "little folks" were all ready; and in three months
from the laying of the keel, the *Morning Star* was in
trim for her long voyage round Cape Horn!

CHAPTER V.

HER VOYAGE AROUND CAPE HORN.

On the evening of November 30th, 1856, a farewell meeting was held in Park Street Church, Boston, at which Captain Moore and his crew were present. Both he and myself were to receive our "instructions," as to where we were to go, and what we were to do. The house was crowded with the friends of the little vessel, who wished to hear what would be said to us.

The first day of winter was cold; but many Christian friends met on board our missionary packet, to bid her and her company "God speed!" It was not, however, till the next day that she spread her white sails for the long voyage. (See the cover.) With deep interest we watched the forms of loved ones, as they stood on the wharves, sending after us their best wishes. When should we see their faces again? Though it was a tender hour, it was a happy one. We thought it a great privilege to be permitted to go to the heathen in such a vessel. Oh, how many prayers were offered by Jesus' little lambs for her preservation!

We sailed beautifully out of Boston harbor; but, not long after, a dreadful storm came upon us. The *Morning Star* was forced to anchor under the lee of Cape Cod, off Provincetown; and so were two other vessels, one on each side of her. The wind shifted during the night; and the next morning we saw our two neighbors high up on the shore, amid the breakers. But God had taken care of us, and the *Morning Star* held fast, and was all safe! There we lay for three days, till a steamer from

Boston came to our assistance; and, having towed us around the Cape, she left us to go on our way over the stormy Atlantic.

When we reached the South Atlantic, we found that our fore-yard was sprung; and so we put into Rio Janeiro for repairs. The harbor was very beautiful, and we enjoyed the visit, to which the nice oranges and bananas added not a little. On the 24th of February, we passed Cape Horn, where we encountered another severe gale. But God helped us, and in a few days we had passed the stormy Cape, where vessels are often detained for weeks.

Soon after entering the Pacific, we felt that the Holy Spirit was with us; and ere we reached the Sandwich Islands, we hoped that some of our company had given their hearts to the Saviour. Our carpenter had been very profane during the early part of the voyage, and, when reasoned with, he thought he could not help swearing. But when he determined to become a Christian, he strove hard and successfully against this great sin. Sometimes he would haul in a rope that might be accidentally dragging in the sea, without being told to do it. And when some of his companions wondered at this, he replied that the vessel belonged to Jesus, and he wished to help take care of it, even if he was not commanded by the officer to do what he knew he ought to do. It made us happy to think that God had blessed the little vessel on her first voyage.

On the 20th of April, 1857, we had our first view of the snow-capped mountains of Hawaii, distant more than a hundred miles. The sunrise was beautiful, the clouds being tinged with a gorgeous crimson, and everything seemed to be in harmony with the feelings of joy which we experienced, when, at about six o'clock, as I was sweeping the western horizon with my glass, the majestic Mauna Kea was distinctly seen! Many hours did we spend that day on deck, awed by the stupendous pile which, so far away from us, was piercing the clouds.

We passed Hawaii on our left; and the next morning we had Maui and Molokai in full view. As we coasted along the shore of the latter, we were charmed with the numerous cascades which rushed down the rocky precipices near the sea.

I shall not soon forget the first sight of Oahu, the island of my birth, with its rugged mountains, cocoa-nut groves, little villages, and, last of all, the beautiful harbor of Honolulu. Many years had rolled away since I had left it, then a mere boy. As we neared the land, a small schooner passed us, and her captain, standing upon her rail, shouted, "Welcome to the *Morning Star!*" And then from the crowd of natives on her deck there went up a round of cheers, which seemed to come from full hearts. These people were very glad to see the *Morning Star*, of which they had heard so much, and toward the building of which many of their children had given their money. The captain who welcomed us was a brother of Dr. Gulick, of Micronesia; and he is now the principal of a Girls' Boarding-School at Waialua, Oahu. He came on board with Mr. Bond, and the watermelon, cocoa-nuts, potatoes, sweet and Irish, which they gave us, were a great luxury, after we had been so many months upon the deep.

We had not been long at Honolulu, when the good people wished to give the *Morning Star* a new flag. At the time it was presented, thousands assembled near the vessel on the wharf; speeches were made, songs were sung, and great joy was expressed in what the children had done. Amid the shouts of the people, the new flag was hoisted to the mast-head by Captain Moore.

CHAPTER VI.

SHE VISITS THE MARQUESAS ISLANDS.

THE *Morning Star* was first sent to the Marquesas Islands, to relieve the wants of the Hawaiian missionaries who were living there. Many years before, English missionaries made some effort to carry the Gospel to the Marquesans ; afterwards American missionaries renewed the attempt ; but none of them saw fit to remain permanently.

In 1853 a chief of one of these islands, Matunui, came to the Sandwich Islands in a whale-ship, with his son-in-law, who was a Hawaiian, to ask for missionaries.   Christians felt that this was a Macedonian cry ; and soon they sent back with him four Hawaiian missionaries and their wives.   The names of the men were Kekela, Kauwealoha,. Kuaihelani, and Kaiwi.   Mr. Bicknell, an Englishman, also went with them, hoping that he might assist them.

The people of Fatuhiva, where Matunui lived, seemed very glad to see him again.   But only five days. after they had landed, a French brig anchored there, bringing a Catholic priest.   He demanded of Matunui and the other chiefs that these missionaries should be sent away, saying that the Marquesas Islands belonged to the French. One of the chiefs replied, " No ; the land is not yours. It belongs to this people ; and there never was a Frenchman born on Fatuhiva ; and these teachers must not be sent back."   So the Hawaiians were not sent away ; and they were very glad, you may be sure, to remain.   Matunui, however, did not always treat them kindly.

In 1856 a vessel was chartered at Honolulu to visit

them, and Dr. Lowell Smith was sent to inquire of their
welfare.   On his return to the Sandwich Islands, he gave
an account of his visit.   " I found our friends," he said,
" all in usual health, cheerful and happy in their work;
but they had been obliged, for several months, to look a
little too much on the 'shady side.'"   You will ask,
perhaps, " What was this ' shady side.' " ?   I will let Dr.
Smith tell you : " Brother Bicknell had sold his hand-
saws, plane-irons, chisels, hatchets, and adze, and one or
two razors, in exchange for food.   And the native missionaries had parted with most of their knives and forks
and spoons, for the same purpose.   They said that they
would soon have been obliged to part with their clothes,
if their supplies had not come to hand."   I am sure that
you will consider these Hawaiians worthy of being fed and
clothed, when you read what Dr. Smith says of them :
" The apparent respect and confidence with which the
natives daily called upon them for favors or advice, re-
minded me of what has occurred around my own door for
the last twenty years."

It was the privilege of Dr. Smith to welcome Natua,
the " first-fruits " of the mission, to the Church of Christ,
giving him the baptismal name of Abraham, because he
was the " father of the faithful " among the Marquesans.
Let me tell you a pleasant story of this good man.   In
1858 a whale-ship visited his island ; and, being on board
of her, he was invited to sit at the cabin-table.   But not
a morsel of food would he taste, till he had asked a blessing.   He tried to speak in English, and said : " O Great
Fader !   Got no fader ; got no moder ; got no broder ;
got no sister !   Make first the sea ; make first the dry
land ; make first the moon and stars ; make first the trees ;
then He make man.   And now, Great Fader, give man
his belly-full.   Amen ! "

You may smile when you read this simple prayer.   But
you remember, do you not, those sweet words of the
Saviour, " She hath done what she could " ?   And Natua

did what *he* could.   What a sublime conception of God
did he express !   Pardon the poor man's English, because
of his great thoughts.

My young friends are glad, I do not doubt, that the
Morning Star could go to visit these good missionaries the
next year, before they should be too much in want.   She
took out two other Hawaiian laborers, Kaukau and his
wife, to help them ; and on her return she brought Mr.
Bicknell to Honolulu, to superintend the printing of the
Gospel of John and other books.

On her way back, she touched at Hilo, on the island
of Hawaii, where Mr. Coan lives, who was for so many
years pastor of the largest church in the world.   Some of
you may remember the letter which he wrote at that time.
Here is a part of it : " The morning of the 7th of July
dawned gloriously on Hawaii.   The mountains were throwing off their night-robes, and adorning themselves in the
light drapery of the dawn ; the fields were slowly unveil-
ing their peerless beauty ; the ocean began to reflect the
first tinges of morning light, when suddenly the sound,
' Hokuao!   (*Morning Star !*) Hokuao!' broke our slum-
bers !   ' Hokuao ! Hokuao !' echoed and reëchoed from
every headland and hill, and rolled back from every val-
ley along our coast ; and multitudes of children waked,
and ran, and shouted, and caught the ' flying joy.'   All
Hilo was active.   Away in the eastern horizon floated
that beauteous Star of Hope, while Venus, like an angel's
eye, looked down upon her from the vault of heaven.
Then we felt that our prayers had been heard, and re-
alized that the sleepless eye of Him who proclaims Himself ' the Bright and Morning Star,' was also looking down
upon that little consecrated bark.   And while our spirit-
ual organs seemed to catch the notes of the celestial
anthem, as ' the morning stars sang together,' our bodily
ears did hear many voices of the ' sons of God,' as they
' shouted for joy.' "

CHAPTER VII.

SHE SETS OUT FOR MICRONESIA.

By the 7th of August the *Morning Star* was ready to start for Micronesia. A farewell meeting was held on board; missionaries, foreigners, and natives crowding her deck. We were commended to the kind care of our heavenly Father, with prayer, both in English and Hawaiian; the "Missionary Hymn" was sung; the benediction was pronounced; the moorings of your little vessel were cast off, and our long voyage of more than twenty thousand miles was resumed, after a pleasant visit of three months, among a people so recently converted from heathenism.

We touched twice at Kauai, one of the Hawaiian Islands, and held pleasant meetings on shore. All were delighted to see us, and to contribute something for our comfort. But this last of Christian lands that we were to see for many years, faded at length in the distance. And yet, as we were wafted farther and farther from the friends we loved, our joy only increased; for we thought, "Soon we shall be proclaiming the love of Christ to those who are sitting in darkness."

After we had been fourteen days without the sight of land, the good chronometer which the Sunday-School children of Essex Street Church, Boston, had given to the *Morning Star*, told us that we were nearing Uderik, one of the Marshall Islands. Oh, how eager I was to catch my first glimpse of a Micronesian island! And do you not think that I was very happy to be the first one to see the cocoa-nut tree tops just rising out of the ocean? With

WELCOME OF THE MORNING STAR.

a burst of joy I shouted, "Land ho!" And instantly the word was taken up by almost all on board, till the fishes around us might have wondered at a sound so new and strange.

We passed near enough to see with the naked eye several specks upon the beach. These, the spy-glass showed us, were human beings. Gladly would we have stopped to tell them of our errand; but we were obliged to pass them by; and even to this day no missionary has landed there. Poor people! Do you not pity them? Perhaps the new vessel will bear the "glad tidings" to them.

Two days later we passed so near Mentchikoff Island that we could see the men, women, and children upon the beach. Some of them waved their mats to us, and we in turn waved our handkerchiefs to them. You will find a picture, illustrating this first welcome of the *Morning Star* by the heathen of Micronesia, on the preceding page.

It was not long before several of them pushed off in a proa to visit us. They were strange-looking men; and the strangest thing about them was the pair of ear-rings which they wore. Only think of having a hole in the lower part of one's ear, large enough to put a man's arm through! Just look at the picture of the Marshall Islander on the opposite page, and you will see what I mean.

The narrow strip around the tortoise-shell ear-ring is a part of the ear itself. The large hole has been made by constant stretching. When the ear-rings are taken out, they often hang it up; in other words, they put the lower part of the ear on the top of the ear. The long hair is firmly tied in a knot on the back of the head, which is sometimes adorned with white lilies and a coronet of shells, curiously wrought. You see that this man is carefully tattooed.

One of the men who came off to us, asked for a knife and tobacco, the latter of which the *Morning Star* had

A MARSHALL ISLANDER.

not for sale. He offered in return mother-of-pearl fish-hooks, nicely contrived and neatly finished, a few cocoa-nuts, and several broken sea-shells.

Not long after this we were visited by another man, who came off to us in a canoe just large enough to carry himself. It was so frail, so old, so leaky, that it seemed as if every wave would swamp it. He had to keep bail-ing it all the while, by means of a skilfully contrived scoop, with which he tossed out the water with great ease and rapidity. I held up to him a file, a jews-harp, and a letter, which I had written at the suggestion of Captain Moore. It read much as follows : —

MORNING STAR, *Aug.* 29, 1857.
S. G. Moore, *Captain.*

To the Inhabitants of Mentchikoff Island :

Glad tidings! "Glory to God in the highest; peace on earth; good-will toward men." "God so loved the world that He gave His only-begotten Son, that whoso-ever believeth in Him, might not perish, but have ever-lasting life."

We hope soon to bring you the Gospel of Jesus Christ, and some of His missionaries to teach you.

Very truly yours,
HIRAM BINGHAM, Jr.,
Missionary to Micronesia.

P. S. — We left Honolulu August 7th, and are bound for Strong's Island.

This man came near enough to take these articles from my hands. The file, however, slipped from him, and he instantly dove after it; but it outstripped him in its bot-tom-ward flight, and he returned without it. The letter, which he still held in his hand, was completely drenched; but he laid it with care upon the little platform between the canoe and its outrigger. I gave him another file; and Captain Moore gave him some fish hooks and hard bread.

After this friendly interview with these natives, we squared our yards for Kusaie, and soon left them astern. Perhaps some of my young friends will ask whether the Marshall Islanders could read the letter which I had written them, and which I may call my first sermon to the Micronesians. We did not suppose that they could ; but we hoped that they would one day show it to some white man, who could tell them of the " glad tidings " which it contained.

---◆---

CHAPTER VIII.

HER VISIT TO KUSAIE.

THOUGH it was only three hundred and fifty miles from Mentchikoff Island to Kusaie, we were ten days in making the passage, owing to head-winds and calms Much of Micronesia is in the " doldrums," as the sailors call the low latitudes; and often, while passing from one island to another, our patience is sorely tried by fitful breezes, ocean-currents, and the torrid sun.

On the 8th of September we dropped anchor in one of the beautiful harbors of Kusaie. What a feast to our weary eyes was this gem of the Pacific, — so green, so romantic, so lovely ! All about us there rose abruptly hills and mountains, covered to their very summits with the densest verdure. Beneath cocoa-nut and bread-fruit and banana and banyan trees nestled the picturesque dwellings of the natives. Here and there a light canoe passed rapidly along, bearing the rich, spontaneous fruits which had only to be gathered as they were needed. Snow-white birds sailed gracefully along, at a dizzy height, toward the dark mountain-sides.

On a lovely islet, which the missionaries called " Dove

8

Island," stood the cottage of Mr. Snow; and not far off were the houses of Dr. Pierson and Kanoa. Oh, how beautiful was this secluded spot! It might have been called a fairy scene. We could not help thinking of the words, —

"Where every prospect pleases."

Too soon, however, we felt the force of those other words, —

"And only man is vile."

A house was pointed out to us, where a few white men and several natives of Rotuma had been for many days blockaded by the Kusaieans. Some of them had designed to kill the king and take the island; and the missionaries had good reason to believe that these reckless men had wished to destroy their lives. But God had mercifully preserved His servants thus far. Before our arrival several of the insurgents had been slain; and others had taken refuge in the house to which I have referred. You will not wonder that our brethren were very glad to see the *Morning Star*, for which they had been looking so earnestly! It was a great relief to them to have the little packet so near them, ready for any emergency. She brought a mail, moreover, that contained tidings of their friends for more than a year.

We soon assembled in Mr. Snow's house to thank our heavenly Father for all his "mercy and truth." And through His gracious influence our little vessel was soon made a peacemaker. A meeting between the king and the leading insurgents was held on board of her; and it was arranged that most of them should leave the island at an early day. Four of the Rotumas we took with us to Ponape.

The king declared that he wanted no white men to remain on his island, except the missionaries. He knew that the latter came, not to kill and to rule, but t

American Board of Commissioners for Foreign Missions.

$.50 — 5 Shares

This certifies that [illegible],
has contributed 5 dimes for the new

MISSIONARY PACKET, MORNING STAR.

Missionary House.
Boston, June 1866.

Langdon S. Ward,
TREAS. A.B.C.F.M.

preach the gospel of peace; and he felt quite willing
to trust them. The missionaries were very glad to
hear him express his confidence in them; and although
scarcely any one had been converted during their five
years of hard labor, they did not think of giving up
and going elsewhere. When Mr. Snow told him of his
purpose to visit Ponape for a few weeks, he seemed re-
luctant to let him go.

We were happy, during the visit, to make the acquaintance of Keduka, one of the earliest converts.
Mr. Snow told a pleasant story about him, in con-
nection with Dr. Pierson's arrival in the *Belle.* He
was away from home on some pressing business, when
he saw a vessel. He immediately left his business, and
hastened to the pilot, to go with him to the ship. "Me
think missionary stop board that ship," he afterward
said to Mr. Snow. "Me want to go 'long pilot; look
quick. Me no care nothing 'bout 'nother ship come
before; but me think missionary in this ship; that's
what for I want go; look plenty." This man is still
one of the leading Christians in the little church on
Kusaie.

Taking Mr. Snow and Dr. Pierson with their families,
we set sail for Ponape, September 15th, to visit the
missionaries there, and to hold a meeting of the Micronesia mission, to decide what new stations should
be occupied, and what men should commence them.

—◆—

CHAPTER IX.

HER VISIT TO PONAPE.

On the 23d of September we entered the Metálanim
harbor, on the east side of Ponape, mountain-locked, like

the one we had just left, with surroundings less abrupt,
indeed, but more grand.   Here too we saw the same intense green ; and on our left we beheld two picturesque
water-falls, which greatly enhanced the beauty of the
place.   On our right, standing by itself, was the " Sugar
Loaf," several hundred feet high ; and were any of you
to see it, you would say at once, " It *is* a Sugar Loaf."
All who visit this place, are struck with the extraordinary
likeness.

At Shalong, near this harbor, was the home of Dr.
Gulick.   We were very glad when he came alongside of
our vessel in his little boat, called the *Soso*.   We had on
board his gray-haired father ; and their meeting, after a
five years' separation, was truly affecting.

Ponape is a much larger island than Kusaie ; and there
were three missionary stations on it.   Word was soon
sent to the other brethren that the *Morning Star* had arrived.   Our friends were delighted to hear the tidings ;
for the food of some of them was nearly gone, and they
found it hard to buy any of the natives.   Indeed, they
were about making their necessities a subject of special
prayer ; when lo !   He who hath " the times and the sea-
sons " in His own hand, sent the missionary ship to them
just at the right time !

Missionary life on Ponape has always been one of much
hardship.   But those who have been sowing in tears, are
now reaping in joy.   Some of the trials which in early
years they were subjected to, will appear in the following
extracts from a letter of Mr. Doane : — " Not a native
boy or girl, man or woman, can we get to do anything for
us.   Our family work I am obliged to share with my wife ;
and my co-laborers do likewise.   I am familiar with the
kitchen and the wash-tub.   All the out-door work, moreover, I must do.   I must go after firewood, bring it home
in a small canoe, and then cut it.   I must bring my own
water ; I must attend to the watering and feeding of my
cow.   I must, in short, help myself, if I would be helped.

And in this hot climate it requires no little energy to go forward, and do all that is needful." And yet this good brother was "not disheartened." He felt, moreover, that his trials might help forward the work which he was doing. "One good result at least," he wrote, "will come from all this. When the natives see us toiling thus, all wet with perspiration, all sore with toil, coats off, perhaps in the water up to the knees, they will see that we have not come here to play the gentleman."

While the *Morning Star* lay in the harbor of Metá-lanim, a meeting was held on board of her, for the sake of giving the missionaries at Shalong a public opportunity to testify their joy, and also to impress upon the natives the nature of the work which she was doing. Captain Moore and others made addresses, which Dr. Gulick interpreted. The flag was exhibited, with other articles of interest, among them a large Bible. The exercises were closed by singing,

"Waft, waft, ye winds, His story," &c.

From Metálanim harbor we proceeded to Mr. Doane's station, in the Jokoij tribe, on the northwest side of the island, to take on board his goods. While this was going on, the Wajai (a high chief) came to Mr. Doane's house, and commenced stoning the people, saying that our missionary brother was leaving them because they did not come to hear him preach on the Sabbath.

He and other chiefs accompanied Mr. Doane to the *Morning Star* in several canoes. For a short time we endeavored to entertain them with instrumental and vocal music. Mr. Doane then implored God's blessing upon them, and bade them "good-bye." You will be glad to know that his labors among that tribe were not in vain. Many of the people, including this very Wajai, are now coming to Jesus.

From this station we proceeded to Ron Kiti, the residence of Mr. Sturges. In his hospitable dwelling we had a pleasant home for a week and more. His house stood upon a high hill, surrounded with bread-fruit, cocoa-nut, and papaw trees, and overlooking the smooth sheet of water where the *Morning Star* lay safely moored.

We enjoyed the few days which we spent on Ponape very much. Those who dwell in Christian lands, can hardly imagine the pleasure which missionaries derive from intercourse with each other. It is " like the precious ointment upon the head, that ran down upon the beard, even Aaron's beard ; that went down to the skirts of his garments." But the time soon came for our parting words. The isles were waiting for the law !

It had been decided to commence new stations on the Marshall and Gilbert Islands. Although there were some five thousand people on Ponape, even after the terrible ravages made by the small-pox, it was thought best to send Dr. Pierson and Mr. Doane to the Marshall Islands, as also Kanoa and myself to the Gilbert Islands. Some of us, therefore, must turn away from these " heavenly places in Christ Jesus," and preach the " unsearchable riches " where they had not been known.

And so, on the 15th of October, we set sail and entered the Metálanim harbor again, to take on board Mrs. Gulick (with three children), who was going to the Sandwich Islands for her health. While attempting to get to sea, the *Morning Star* struck on one of the thousand reefs with which these waters abound, where she thumped about for ten or fifteen minutes ; but the Keeper of Israel mercifully cared for us ; and before night we were safely under way. Dr. Gulick then left us to return in his little boat to his " hermit-home," while we bore away for Eastern Micronesia. You will not wonder that he called to mind the following words : —

" Thou who dost the winds control,
Guide our vessel to her goal;
Pour the sunshine o'er her track;
Father, lead the storm-cloud back.

"Infant hopes are centred there,
Infant voices raised in prayer;
Infant hands have launched the bark;
Safely speed thee, Gospel Ark!"

———◆———

CHAPTER X.

HER VISIT TO APAIANG.

WE touched at Wellington and McAskill Islands, and then at Kusaie to return Mr. and Mrs. Snow to their home, henceforth to be so lonely, in consequence of the removal of Dr. Pierson and Kanoa. With the latter were two Gilbert Islanders, a man and his wife, who had drifted away from their own group. They had taught Kanoa a few words of their language, which were of much use to him in beginning his new work.

Your missionary vessel was now loaded down as much as she could be with safety ; for she had on her decks (besides much of the lumber for my little framed house which I took out from Honolulu) poles and posts for building houses, as soon as possible, upon the new islands to which the other missionaries were going.

Though the *Morning Star* sailed from Kusaie for the Gilbert Islands, she was compelled by the winds to pass near Ebon. Of our exciting interview with the people there, I will tell you in the next chapter.

It was on the 13th of November that I climbed almost to the top of the mast, and caught the first sight of what proved to be, for so many years, our island-home. It was Apaiang, a low coral reef, some fifty miles in circumference, enclosing one of those great lagoons which I have already described. The highest parts of this reef were only a few feet above the ocean ; but on these were many cocoa-nut and pandanus trees. The lowest parts were covered with

water at high tide. The lagoon was about eighteen miles
long, six wide, and one hundred feet deep. The land
surrounding it did not average more than a quarter of a
mile in width ; but on this narrow strip, such 'as it was,
were many villages.

We landed first on an islet, belonging to the western side, where the reef is lowest. There we found a
solitary old man, walking among the trees. He was the
first Gilbert Islander to receive the missionaries, who had
come to live among his people ! On the 17th of November the *Morning Star* entered the beautiful lagoon, and
came to anchor near Koinawa, the king's village, on the
eastern side.

Next morning the king, at our request, came on board,
and, learning something of our wishes from the Gilbert
Islanders with us, he seemed pleased ; and, putting .his
hand on me and on my lumber, he pointed to the shore.
I took the hint, and the very next day we began to build.
The house was twenty-four feet by sixteen, and though
we took time to shingle it, much to the wonder of the
natives, in less than two weeks it had been made so comfortable as to be ready for housekeeping. We afterwards
painted it white, except the blinds, which were green, and
put on piazzas. We called it " Happy Home."

In the picture of the station, on the opposite page, it is
the largest building on the right. On the left is Kanoa's
house, somewhat like it, but made chiefly of cocoa-nut
wood, with pandanus thatch for roofing. The buildings
from which you see smoke issuing are our kitchens. You
notice that they have no chimneys, and the smoke escapes
through openings in the gable-ends. Back of Kanoa's
house stands a school-house, which we built for the pupils
of Mrs. Bingham and Kaholo.

The water in the foreground is a part of the lagoon.
See that poor woman dragging a canoe along the shore,
in which her husband sits, leisurely smoking a pipe. The
wind is ahead ; but little does he care how hard she must

toil beneath the burning sun to tow him, as if she were a mule or donkey, to his home, some five or six miles away. Oh, how much woman, in this Christian land, owes to the Gospel! A part of this picture serves to illustrate what is mentioned on page   .

On the 2d of December, 1857, just one year from the day of *our* departure from Boston, the *Morning Star* was ready to take *her* departure from Apaiang. And now we were to be left alone among these savages! Would they treat us kindly? Or would they steal from us, and perhaps murder us? Could we live happily among them? Should we not be very lonely? By remaining on board our little vessel, we might be carried again to dear friends. What, think you, were our thoughts in such an hour? We were glad to remain, to teach the people, and to lead them to Jesus. And while we loved your missionary packet, in which we had sailed so many thousand miles, we would not detain her longer. Getting into my little canoe, I paddled off to the shore, while the children's messenger of peace went her way on other errands of love. From that time forward, we were to have no American fellow-laborers, and yet we were not alone. The Saviour. as He had promised, was with us!

CHAPTER XI.

HER VISIT TO EBON.

EBON is one of the Marshall Islands, all of which are coral reefs. As more rain falls on them than on the Gilbert Islands, they are much more fertile, and abound, not only in cocoa-nuts and the fruit of the pandanus or screw-pine, but also in bread-fruit, and a variety of the taro, the last being a vegetable which is used much as we me potatoes. Some bananas are also raised. Neither goats, nor sheep, nor cattle, as I have said, can live on either the Marshall or Gilbert Islands; and of course the natives never have any fresh beef or mutton or milk or butter. But in both groups dogs and rats abound, and there are some cats and fowls. Land-birds are scarce, but sea-birds are plenty everywhere.

The Marshall Islanders are bold navigators, and frequently set out in their proas, without any compass, for small islands distant a hundred miles. Sometimes they get adrift, however, and wander about over the ocean for weeks, before they find a landing-place.

It was in this way that the party of which I have spoken in another place, drifted to Kusaie, in a starving condition, and fully expecting to be put to death. But they were treated kindly, and permitted to return to their homes in peace. God had commanded the winds to take them to that distant island, that they might see what the missionaries were doing, and so be ready to welcome them. Some of these were among the people whom we met, as I have said, when sailing from Kusaie to Apaiang. We had heard much of their barbarity; for they had made a covenant of death, and had resolved that every white man who should set his foot upon their island, should be killed! Only a little while before, indeed, a vessel had been seized by them, and all the crew slain.

And now, as we saw one large proa suddenly shoot out from the lagoon, and then another and another, (in spite of the roughness of the sea,) we began to fear lest our little vessel might be seized also. What then was our sense of relief, when, as Dr. Pierson addressed the first proa that reached us in the language of Ebon, the man who was steering recognized him, and exclaimed, repeatedly, and with great joy, " Doketur! (Doctor) Doketur! Mitchinari! (missionary) Mitchinari!" All in the canoe became highly excited, laughing most joyously. The news soon spread like wildfire among the fleet of seven-

teen proas. Some of the natives soon boarded us, and
when they learned that Dr. Pierson was expecting to return in the course of one or two " moons," they were
greatly delighted. See a picture of this scene on the
title-page.

We felt that " the set time to favor " them had come,
and that the God of missions had prepared the way for
His servants. Kaibuke, the head chief, welcomed the
missionaries on their return from Apaiang, assuring them
again that their lives and property should be perfectly
safe. He told them to select any place on the island
which they might prefer. He called Dr. Pierson his son,
and said that any injury done to him would be regarded
as done to himself. They soon chose a spot upon which
to build, called by the people " Rube," and they were
much pleased with the cheerfulness of the natives while
assisting them in putting up their houses.

The missionaries were happy in the prospect before
them, as you will judge from what Mr. Doane wrote at
that time. " Let me be a missionary," he said, " a pioneer
missionary, if my Master so wills it, and I ask no other,
no higher employment in this world. To enter in among
a people, lost, depraved, exposed to endless ruin, and tell
them of the way of life, of the blessed Saviour, of the
riches of his dying love, — this is all and the only work
I ask for in this life."

The Marshall Islanders have been very treacherous until recently, and even now it might not be safe for white
men to live on some of the islands. But Dr. Pierson, Mr.
Doane, and their wives, were not afraid to be left by the
Morning Star; and after their houses had been partially
built, the vessel set out for Honolulu, Christmas, 1857.
But it was a great comfort to them, I can assure you, (as
it was to all of us,) that the Morning Star was to return
next year.

CHAPTER XII.

WAITING FOR THE MORNING STAR.

As soon as we were left upon Apaiang, we began to learn the language which we were to use; but, as none of the people spoke English, it was slow work. One word after another we picked up, by pointing to this thing and that, by representing various motions, as rising up, walking, sitting down, throwing, and so on. The little children delighted in counting their fingers for us, that we might learn to count as they did. And this was what they said: "Teuana, uoua, tenua, aua, nimaua, onoua, itua, wanua, ruaiua, tebwina." Would you have ever dreamed that they were saying, "One, two, three, four," &c.?

We had hardly been in our new home three months, when a party of Gilbert Islanders from Tarawa, not far off, made an attack upon our people in a fleet of one hundred proas. Our king assembled his army about our house to await the onset, as the other party seemed to be coming directly towards us. They changed their course, however, and the battle was fought some six miles away. The king who had befriended us when we landed, was killed, but his people were victorious.

Next morning I visited the battle-ground; and there I saw among the dead six women, who had helped their husbands in the fight. We were very sorry that so many had been killed; but we were thankful that the savages had been driven off; for it is quite possible that they might have slain us, and taken possession of our little house.

And here I must explain the engraving on the next leaf. It represents two Gilbert Island warriors, going to battle. Formerly this people had no guns, but fought with clubs and spears; and even now they like to take their old weapons into battle with them, to use when their

powder is gone. Some of the spears are armed with
sharks' teeth, and are almost twenty feet long. To pro-
tect themselves they have a kind of armor, made of
cocoa-nut fibre cord. A part of this resembles a great-
coat; and it comes up behind their heads, to shield them
from behind, or when they run. They also make cover-
ings for their legs, arms, and head, of the same material,
and still another covering for the head, of the skin of the
porcupine-fish. The picture opposite is quite lifelike.

The *Morning Star* will not be here for some time.
Let me take you, therefore, on a missionary tour. We
put up some bread and boiled salt-beef; a little rice, and
a little butter, if we have any; a saucepan, a keg of
water from our well, for the water in most wells is very
bad. We take a mat, a blanket or two, and loading up
our little boat, which we call the *Alfred*, (for we have
neither carriages, nor horses, nor mules, nor donkeys, you
know,) we set off for a heathen village.

A crowd of naked men, boys, and girls meet us as we
land; and we go directly to the *maneaba* of the village.
The people throng about us; and we try to teach them
to sing and pray, and we speak of Jesus' love. As we
close our eyes for prayer, one and another shout to those
near them, " Matu, matu! " (" Go to sleep; go to
sleep! ") meaning, " Shut your eyes." After a general
commotion, in which some bow their faces to the ground,
the prayer is offered. At its close, as the missionary
opens his eyes, a number begin to shout, " Uti, uti! "
(" Wake up, wake up! ") and, with a burst of laughter,
these rude worshippers sit up again.

I begin to preach. But the leading man of the village
may break in upon me, by asking if I will not take a
pipe. " I never smoke," is the answer. Next he may
offer me some molasses and water to drink, or the milk
of a green cocoa-nut. Sometimes we tell them that we
have not come to eat and drink, but to teach them. It
is often better, however, to stop preaching, and drink

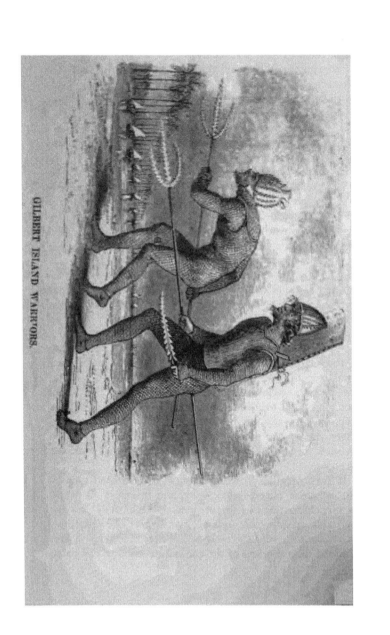

GILBERT ISLAND WARRIORS.

from the cocoa-nut, and then go on again. After service
we often look up the blind and sick of the village, and
teach them in their own houses.

We go to the next village. Perhaps we find the
maneaba preoccupied. A man has died, and his body
has been brought to the big house, and is laid out in state.
Women sit by it, day after day, even for weeks. You
will wonder how they *can* do so, especially in such a hot
climate. Poor creatures! They think that in this way
they are treating the dead man kindly. Most of the
time the body is covered by a mat; and frequently beneath the same mat lies the dead man's wife, grieving
over her loss. When at length the corpse is about to be
buried, the wife often keeps his skull, and makes it her
constant companion. (See the right-hand figure in the
picture on page 51.)

A man is generally buried under his own house, and
only a few inches below the surface of the ground; for
the people think that if there should be room for another
corpse above him, there would soon *be* another to fill the
place. Sometimes, however, bodies are rolled up in
mats, and laid away in a loft of the house.

When we find the *maneaba* thus occupied, the friends
of the deceased are usually willing to listen to me while I
urge them to prepare for death. But sometimes we find
the people assembled for a feast. If they have only
cocoa-nut milk to drink, or cocoa-nut molasses and water,
they are generally willing to hear me speak of the land
where men never hunger; and yet they may be very
desirous to know what kind of food they may expect
there.

If the people are drinking *mang'ing*, (fermented toddy,)
some of them may be very noisy, and interrupt us while
we preach to them of temperance. When they are intoxicated, they often quarrel, and kill one another;
sometimes they stab themselves. When the toddy is first
obtained from the bud of the cocoa-nut, which is cut twice

a day, it is pleasant and wholesome. But if it is allowed to
stand three or four days, it ferments and becomes hurtful.
A great deal of it. nevertheless, is drunk in the Gilbert
Islands ; and they need missionaries to teach them better.
When night overtakes us, we spread our mats on
the ground, hang up our musquito-netting in some
native house, and lie down to sleep. In the morning,
perhaps, while we are eating the food which we have
brought, the people will crowd around us, saying, " Kamai
teutana," (" Give me a little piece.") If we refuse them,
they may call us " bataoti," (" stingy.") But we could
not give all of them even a little piece ; if we should, our
supply would soon be gone.

After several days have been spent in this way, the tour
is completed, and we spread our sail for the white cottage
among the cocoa-nut trees. As we cross the lagoon, we
enjoy an hour of rest, which is very refreshing.

But some bright-eyed boy may say, " You have taken
us on a preaching tour, but you have not told us *when* and
where you began to preach at home." Well, I will say
a word on this point just here. I had been living on
Apaiang about six months, when I began to address the
natives publicly in their own tongue. At first I spoke to
them in the *maneaba* of Koinawa, a large village near us
where the king lives. This building answered the purpose
of a chapel very well ; still we thought it best to build a
small church, to be dedicated to the worship of the true
God.

You have a picture of this building on the next
leaf. We are going to church, you see ; and Kanoa, my
Hawaiian associate, is blowing a shell, to call the people
to meeting, as we have no bell. Kanoa's wife, with one
of her children, is just behind us. Be sure to look at
the king, son of the one who was killed, in his long
shirt, and under his umbrella. The queen will come too,
for both are very regular in their attendance ; and, what
is better still, we hope they are Christians.

4

You will say, perhaps, that some things in this picture look more like breaking the Sabbath than keeping it; and you are quite right. You will learn from the scene, however, how the Gilbert Islanders dishonor God's holy day. How much they need the Gospel!

But let me proceed with my explanation. The woman whom you see is a heathen, carrying her husband's skull as she goes on a visit to some other village. A party of the natives are pressing scraped cocoa-nuts in an oil-press, to get the oil to buy tobacco with. The dog is one of the many, as heathenish as their masters, which greatly annoy us.

Three men are climbing cocoa-nut trees in as many different ways. The one at the right has notches cut in his tree, large enough to hold the second joint of the great toe. He is going after his toddy, which he will give his child instead of milk, as they have no cows or goats. The man in the middle walks up the tree in a wonderful way. If one of his hands should slip, he would fall, and perhaps break his neck. The man at the left has his feet tied together, a few inches apart; and while he holds himself away from the tree by pushing off with one arm, and clasping the other round the trunk, he draws up his feet, which easily cling to the tree by the help of the cord which binds them together; and then he straightens himself up again. The second way of climbing is the most difficult. On the right you will see a pandanus-tree. How strange its roots, which grow out of the trunk, and run off into the ground! How large the great bunches of fruit! They sometimes weigh forty or fifty pounds. When they are ripe, you can pull them to pieces, each piece being a separate conical seed some three inches long, the small end of which is fibrous, and contains a sweet juice, is chewed, and the juice is sucked out. See the great papai leaves, back of the chapel, coming up out of a pit! You would call them giant calla leaves. The papai is a root which grows in the

SUNDAY MORNING ON APAIANG.

mud, and is sometimes as large as a half-barrel. The natives eat it as a luxury.

The houses of the natives on the left have, you see, no sides, and the eaves are very low. We must always stoop to enter them, but, when we have once entered, we can see what the people are doing in the next man's house, and so on, through the village. The hut in the distance is a kitchen where poor old women are compelled to do the cooking, half-smothered by the smoke.

—♦—·

CHAPTER XIII.

HER YEARLY VISITS.

THE annual return of the *Morning Star* was always looked forward to with great interest. It would be difficult to say who of the missionaries wished to see her most; but I can assure my young readers that some of the most joyous days of my life were those on which she hove in sight.

The heathen children soon learned how we felt, when the time of her arrival drew near. As soon as a sail was seen in the distant horizon, a shout of " Te ro ! " (" Sail ho ! ") was set up. Our waiting ears were not long in catching the sound, and immediately we sprang for the spy-glass. With almost breathless suspense it was directed to the far-off vessel. For a moment everybody kept still. If the " white flag " was seen at the mast-head, we were sure that she was coming ; and shouts of joy, the clapping of hands, and happy faces, gave indications of the hearty welcome we were ready to give her. A large white flag, with the word WELCOME upon it, was speedily flung to the breeze from a pole tied to the top of a lofty cocoa-nut tree ; and the missionaries' wives

made haste to prepare shore-comforts for the weary voy-
agers.   The picture on page 41 will give you an imperfect
idea of the scene.

Kanoa and myself, launching our little *Alfred*, went out
to meet the *Morning Star* in mid-lagoon.   Oh, what
moments were those during which we watched the dear
vessel, as steadily, but surely, we came nearer and nearer
to each other!   Whom shall we greet on board?   The
same kind captain, or some new face?   What missionaries shall we find, coming to help us?   What missionary father from the Sandwich Islands will counsel
and encourage us?   What shall we hear of fathers and
mothers, brothers and sisters?   Are they yet alive?
And that wicked Rebellion!   What battles have there
been?   What victories and what defeats?   Oh, this
dreadful suspense, when the life of our father-land is in
peril!

And then there was the large mail-bag, with its many
letters from the many friends who had remembered us in
our loneliness.   We had hardly time to think of the good
things to eat which the children's vessel had brought us, —
the flour and salt-beef, and potatoes, sweet and Irish, (we
had eaten none for months,) the watermelons, the bananas, the oranges, the nice jars of jelly and cans of
fruit which loving friends (God bless them!) had sent us.
And the new clothes, and shoes, and umbrellas, were
worth thinking of, had there not been so many other
things of more value.

And now, as the beautiful vessel sails past our boat, a
line is thrown to us.   In a moment we are on board, and
then the hearty shakes of the hand, the searching glances
for familiar faces, the thrilling items of news!   In a few
moments we are at anchor off the mission premises.
Friends go down with us into our little boat; the mail-
bag and a few packages are put in, with a pail of potatoes
for immediate use; and we pull for the shore.

Our wives watch us with intense earnestness, to see if

they can recognize those who have come so many hundreds of miles to our island home. The natives crowd down to the beach to meet us : and, taking up one parcel after another, go with us to the humble cottage of the missionary. and almost immediately fill every place available for sitting. Perhaps the missionary's wife welcomes to her door the first white woman that she has seen in nearly two years. The Hawaiian missionaries assemble with us, and thanks are returned to God for bringing the *Morning Star* once more to us in safety.

Such hours of meeting are precious, and words fly rapidly. The captain and friends visit our little schools, or attend worship in our chapel. In due time our supplies are landed : our mail to friends is put on board : and the little vessel takes her leave, to be absent again for many long, long months. Happy, golden hours ! Bright sunbeams through the thick clouds of isolation ! How soon they are gone ! But our hearts are refreshed. and we gird ourselves anew for the work before us.

Once in two years we join the vessel, to go with her to Ponape. distant one thousand miles, to attend the meeting of the Micronesia mission. This absence of two months. much of the time being spent on board the *Morning Star*. renews our acquaintance with the little craft that brought us to our Micronesian home. We think often of those dear children that desired to help us in our blessed work of telling the heathen of the Lord Jesus Christ.

As we draw near the different stations. where our fellow-missionaries dwell, we often say, " How little do these dear friends know where the *Morning Star* is just now; and how soon their hearts will overflow with joy ! " And how little did *we* know whether our friends were alive or not ! For a whole year, perhaps, we had heard no tidings of them, so little intercourse is there between these islands. How eagerly did we watch the canoes, as they came to meet us, to see if they contained a brother missionary !

I well remember the sad news which we told to one brother, as he boarded us. His wife had died in Honolulu, months before! He had been waiting seven months for a vessel, which left him on Ponape, intending to call in five weeks, and take him to his invalid companion.

———◆———

CHAPTER XIV.

SOME THINGS SHE BROUGHT, AND HOW WE USED THEM.

In this chapter I wish to tell you about a few of the good things which the *Morning Star* brought us. One of these was a nice surf-boat, which we called the *Star of Peace.* It was mainly purchased with money given to us by Captain Moore and his crew, when they took leave of us in December, 1857.

We had visited every part of Apaiang in the little *Alfred;* and we had even crossed in her to Tarawa, the largest island of the group, being towed by one of the great war-proas, which was bearing presents from our king to a high chief, whose two sons had been recently betrothed to two of his daughters.

But there were other islands which could not be reached in our small boat, and on which the Gospel had never been preached. To these we longed to go. One of them could be seen from the top of the cocoa-nut trees near our house; but the ocean channel was more than twenty miles wide, and the current often so swift as to make it very unsafe to venture across in the *Alfred.*

We were very glad, therefore, when the new surf-boat arrived in the *Morning Star*, and still more glad were we, when Captain Gelett said, after he had helped me rig it, that he thought I might safely cross to Marakei and Maiana; for he thought that I was a pretty good sailor.

You may be sure that I was anxious to be off as soon as possible. I went first to Tarawa, where I left Mrs. Bingham, and then to Maiana. On my return from the latter, I had a much harder time than I expected. The wind was favorable when I started ; but it changed afterwards, and we were greatly at the mercy of a current which was very strong. At sundown, Tarawa bore due east, about twelve miles. The wind lulled, but the sea was rough, and we were fast drifting to the westward. A fearful hour was that ! No land to the leeward for more than two hundred miles ! I was in just the place where Mr. Huntley went adrift, on attempting to return to Maiana, after the battle of February 19, 1858. He was picked up thirty days later, all his companions having starved to death. We had food and water to sustain life for a month ; but there are times when no ship can beat up against this current.

At length, however, by dint of hard rowing, we got into stiller water, under the lee of Tarawa ; and a little after midnight, we made out to reach the island. You will not wonder that we were truly joyful and thankful for our escape, from what seemed to be very great danger.

I had sometimes seen Marakei from the top of a cocoanut tree, and I longed to preach the Gospel there. A boat like the *Star of Peace* can seldom cross thither ; but one day everything seemed to be favorable, and Kanoa and myself were soon under way. Now if you will turn to Acts xxvii. 13-15, you will see that the weather may seem to be very good for a voyage, and yet, " not long after," " a tempestuous wind " may arise. This was precisely our case. About three o'clock in the afternoon a fearful squall approached. As we were out on a wide sea, anxious to reach, before night, a strange island, with no ship channel to its lagoon, I kept on sail to the last moment, bidding one of the men " stand by the halyards," and let them go at an instant's warning.

At length I could venture no longer. We lowered

and furled our sails, and had hardly seated ourselves,
when the tempest burst upon us with tremendous fury.
As soon as it abated, we reefed our mainsail, and, hoisting
it up a little, pushed on.   The sea was beginning to run
wildly, and the large billows raised their white crests
around us.   The *Star of Peace* had experienced no such
sea as that.   Suddenly a towering wave burst upon us,
drenching us from stem to stern.   Blinded by the spray,
for the moment I hardly knew our fate.   Thanks to our
kind Keeper, the boat still danced on.   But frightened
faces turned towards me, as if to read the future in my
countenance.

Just at dark, it being difficult to distinguish people on
the shore, we found ourselves off a narrow break in the
cocoa-nut and pandanus trees.   This was the so-called
boat channel, a fearful place, with billows dashing their
foam against the rocks.   I trembled to enter, and would
not venture myself at the helm, lest I should not understand the rapid commands of the pilot, but put my old
teacher at that post, and took his oar.   For a moment we
paused, as the billows began to lift their crests before
breaking.   Two large ones passed, and we sprang to our
oars.   In the darkness, our pilot had " headed-in " a little
too soon, and in order to enter a gap between the rocks,
not forty feet wide, was obliged to slant our course a little,
— a most perilous feat !   For an instant death seemed
staring me in the face.   Swimmer that I was, should we
swamp, the chances for my escape were exceedingly small,
as I was not accustomed to surf-swimming.   But the
blessed Master was with us.   A small wave took us upon
its crest, and we were hurried through this narrow vortex
in a moment's time.

But what a sight greeted our eyes the next morning !
We found ourselves upon one of the loveliest of all the
coral islands.   About six miles in length, from one to
three in width, and enclosing a placid lagoon on all sides
by wooded land, with fairy-like islets here and there, it

lay spread out before us. The Gospel light for the first
time now beamed upon it. We preached in all its
villages; and more than a thousand souls heard of the
way of life.

In passing out of this lagoon, there was quite as much
peril as there had been in passing in. But I will not
describe the scene. Possibly you may think that my
zeal for ocean touring in an open boat was by this time
slightly cooled, or. at least, that it ought to have been.
But it is hard to see a populous island without the Gospel,
and not do anything for it.

Wishing to make this part of our work safer, the Sabbath School children of California sent us a larger boat
than the *Star of Peace*, called the *Evening Star*. You
will see a picture of her on the last page of the cover.
We thank these children very much for their generous
gift.

On page 17 you can see a picture of the *Star of
Peace*. The scene is intended to illustrate our arrival
at a heathen village. We are bound to the *maneaba*.
Kanoa is the man with the umbrella. Do you see the
little boys who are running towards us? They wish to
find out why the *I-matang* (foreigners) have come; but
perhaps they will stay and play with our boat, instead of
going with us to be taught. At the left is a stout man
carrying home a heavy load of cocoa-nuts and pandanus
fruit on a stick across his shoulder, as neither he nor his
friends have a cart or wheelbarrow.

Among other " worthy deeds " of the *Morning Star*,
she has carried printing-presses to Micronesia. The story
of our press at Apaiang I think will please you.

Nearly five years after we landed there, we sent a copy
of the Gospel of Matthew in the Gilbert Island language
to Honolulu, by the hands of Kanoa, to be printed there.
as also a small hymn-book. Thirteen months later,
Kanoa returned in the *Morning Star*, bringing back an
edition of the hymn-book, but no printed copy of Matthew.

We were very sorry, for we had often told our pupils that they would soon have an entire Gospel.

It happened that a printing-press had just been sent to us in the *Morning Star*: and so we said, " We can print Matthew for ourselves." The box which was supposed to contain the press was landed, and soon opened. We found in it a small box of types, cases, and other things used in printing, but no press! The captain felt sure that all had been landed: but I could not rest until I had boarded the vessel and inquired of the mate. He assured me that there was nothing more. As I paddled home that evening, my heart was doubly heavy, from this second disappointment.

Next morning the examination of one of our schools was held; and while this was going on, the captain came to inform me that another search for the missing press was to be made; and, in case it should be found, the Stars and Stripes would be hoisted. How great was our joy, upon leaving the school-house, to see the old flag at the mast-head!

The *Morning Star* soon left us. We had a press, but no printer. A book, however, telling us how to print had been sent, and we hoped soon to understand the business. Only two days after Captain James's departure, a boat entered our lagoon, which had gone adrift with several sailors, when trying to reach a small guano island, some forty miles from the place where they had been wrecked. For ten days they were upon the ocean, and after a voyage of six hundred miles they reached Maiana.

They rested one night, and then set out for Apaiang, in the hope of finding the *Morning Star*, and going in her to Honolulu. The current was too strong, and the wind too much ahead; so they put back, and remained five days longer. They then set out again for Apaiang, and reached us just too late! A few weeks later they had an opportunity of leaving for Sydney in a cocoa-nut oil trader.

One of the men was a printer, and he was willing to remain, and set our little press to work. In a few weeks we had Matthew ready for our pupils! Mr. Hotchkiss (for that was his name) also printed several other small books, which were greatly needed. We love to think that God sent that kind printer to us over the wide ocean, in an open boat, to help us in giving the Word of Life to the poor Gilbert Islanders.

CHAPTER XV.

MICRONESIANS WHO SAILED IN HER.

LET me tell you about some of the Micronesians who have sailed in the *Morning Star.* I will first speak of Joseph, from whom I once expected a great deal, but who afterwards disappointed me. Still I do not give him up. I often pray that he may return to the path of duty and usefulness; and I want you to pray for him too.

Only thirteen letters (a, e, i, o, u, b, k, m, n, ṅ, (ng), r, t, w) are needed for writing the Gilbert Island language. We had taught a few children to spell ba, be, &c., when one day I heard a lad whom we had never taught saying over with great rapidity, " Ba, be, bi, bo, bu ; ka, ke, ki, ko, ku ; ma, me," &c. I was much pleased, for I thought to myself, " This boy must be very bright;" and indeed he *was* very bright. We took great pains to teach him; and soon he learned to read and write his own language very fast.

After a while he came to live with us, with the consent of his father, a brother of the old king that welcomed us to Apaiang. We taught him English also, in the hope that he would be more useful as an assistant translator of the New Testament. But he made some curious mistakes.

He could not easily distinguish between *b* and *p*, and when he tried to read the words, " big pig," he would frequently say, " pig big." Other Gilbert Islanders would have done the same thing.

He took much interest in the various generals who were fighting to save our country, and he knew the names of several of them. On one occasion he saw in large letters, in an advertisement, the words, " General Merchandise." Having spelled them out, he asked, " Does this General command troops? " Ekeuea (for such was his heathen name) helped us very much in learning his language. After we had been at Apaiang a good while, I offered him a cent a word for all the new words he would define for us. In a few months he had give us nearly a thousand !

As he learned about the love of Jesus, he seemed very much interested ; and we had good reason to think him a Christian. At his baptism he chose the name of Joseph, or, as it is written in his language, Ióteba.

We took him with us on one of our voyages to Kusaie and Ponape. He thought the Marshall Islanders hideous-looking people, with their great ear-rings and knotted hair. Their language he called " jabber." His wonder at the mountains of Kusaie (for he had never seen so much as a hill before) was very great. I rambled with him through the woods and by the running streams, of which there are none in the Gilbert Islands ; and together we climbed, with great difficulty, to the top of the highest mountain. The story of this ascent he never wearied in telling his people, after his return.

One night we heard loud crying ; and we supposed it to come from some heathen child. The next morning Joseph told us that he had dreamed of seeing a savage cut off my head ; and, as he awoke, the dream seemed so real, that he arose, left his little house, and sat under the cocoa-nut trees at the dead of night, to give vent to his sorrow.

He often went with me on my tours to assist in telling
the people about Jesus; and they always liked to hear
him. His help too, in translating portions of the New
Testament, was very great. He once visited Butaritari
and Makin, islands where I had never preached, and,
gathering many of the people together, told them the
great news of salvation through Jesus Christ. The journal
which he kept was very interesting.

After a time a white man gave him some liquor, and he
became intoxicated. From that day he left us; perhaps
he is still wandering. Will not my young friends pray
that he may be brought back to the true fold? My heart
yearns over him.   .

But let me speak of another Micronesian, whose history
is more cheering, and who is now at rest with the Lord
Jesus. When Mr. Snow removed from Kusaie to Ebon,
in 1862, he left some thirty converts behind, with many
others who loved him very much. It was a sad day for
them, as I well remember, when he went on board the
Morning Star. Many of them followed him in their
canoes for a mile or two. At length they said their last
" good-byes," and returned to their island-home, as sheep
without a shepherd. But one of the good women, the
wife of Keduka, said in her simplicity that Jesus would be
their missionary now; and her words have been fulfilled.
He has, in very deed, taken care of them; and you will
be glad to know that your little packet has several times
carried Mr. Snow to them, to spend a few days, while she
should be gone to Ponape. It has been very pleasant for
him to make these visits; for he has always found new
converts desirous of being baptized. Shall not this encourage us to plant the Gospel on every island of Micronesia ? ˊ

Mr. Snow took with him to Ebon a young Christian
named Selpas, to aid in making some translations, which
he desired to complete for the Kusaieans. He was
very helpful, and he set a good example of Christian liv-

MR. SNOW'S DEPARTURE FROM KUSAIE.

ing before the natives of Ebon. At length he became
sick, and was glad to return to Kusaie before he should
die. When near his native island, and very feeble, Mr.
Snow asked him where he wanted most to be, expecting
him to say, " In Kusaie." He replied, " In heaven." Mr.
Snow then asked whom he most desired to see, thinking
the answer would be, " My mother; " but it was " Jesus."
He was spared to reach Kusaie, and to see his mother for
a few hours. Then he was taken to his home above ; and
there he looks upon the face of the Blessed One, singing
doubtless, (as he was wont to do so sweetly upon earth,
but oh, how much more sweetly now,) —

> " Okasak sunik on nu mwo,
> On nu sin Leum su es la ko;
> El lunsel sa in on nu sel
> Lun kulan Leum ma mwo nu lal."

> (" Awake, my soul, to joyful lays,
> And sing the great Redeemer's praise;
> He justly claims a song from me,
> His loving kindness, oh, how free.")

On the preceding page is a picture of Mr. Snow's departure from the beautiful home of Selpas. The *Morning
Star* is seen coming out of the harbor, of which I have
spoken as so picturesque, and where at least two whale-
ships have been wrecked in trying to put to sea. In her
wake is the fleet of native Christians, sadly following their
teacher and friends as far as they dare.

CHAPTER XVI.

HER LAST VISIT TO THE MARQUESAS ISLANDS.

I MUST now speak of the last visit of the *Morning Star*
to the Marquesas Islands. Besides her usual freight, she

took out two guns, two gold watches, two silver medals and other things, a gift from President Lincoln. "But how came she, a missionary vessel, to carry such things to a heathen land," you ask, "and that too from our good President?" I will tell you.

An American whale-ship having touched at the Marquesas Islands for supplies, the first mate (Mr. Whalon) went ashore; whereupon he was seized and dragged away. Why? That he might be killed and eaten! But what had he done? Nothing. Wicked men from Peru had landed there, and stolen a number of the Marquesans, to make slaves of them. One of these poor creatures was the son of a chief. The father, of course, was very angry. He was so angry, indeed, that he resolved to kill and eat the first white men who should fall into his hands. And now the day of vengeance had come. The mate was in his power! Others would have fallen into the same snare, but for a Marquesan girl, living in the family of Kekela, (mentioned in Chapter III.,) who made signs to them to go back to their vessel, crying out, "Pull away! pull away!"

Kekela and others made haste to rescue the mate. At first the wrathful chief refused to give up his victim; but he yielded at length to Kekela's entreaties, and offered to receive as a ransom his new six-oared boat, given him by his benefactor in Boston, which he greatly prized, and greatly needed in his missionary work. But the good man did not hesitate a moment to accept the hard terms. Another chief interfered, however, and satisfied the fierce cannibal with a gun and some other things. This story was told to our kind-hearted President; and from his own money, it is said, he gave five hundred dollars to be distributed among Mr. Whalon's deliverers.

You would be glad, I doubt not, to see the letter which Kekela wrote to Mr. Lincoln; but I have room for only a part of it: —

5

" Greetings to you, great and good Friend ! "

" My mind is stirred up to address you in friendship."
" I · greatly respect you for holding converse with such
humble ones. Such you well know us to be." " When
I saw one of your · countrymen, a citizen of your great
nation, ill-treated, and about to be baked and eaten, as a
pig is eaten, I ran to deliver him, full of pity and grief at
the evil deed of these benighted people."

" As to this friendly deed of mine in saving Mr. Whalon,
its seed 'came from your great land, and was brought by
certain of your countrymen, who had received the love
of God. It was planted in Hawaii, and I brought it to
plant in this land and in these dark regions, that they
might receive the root of all that is good and true, which
is *love.*

" 1. Love to Jehovah.

" 2. Love to self.

" 3. Love to our neighbor."

" This is a great thing for your great nation to boast
of, before all the nations of the earth. From your great
land a most precious seed was brought to the land of
darkness."

" How shall I repay your great kindness to me ? Thus
David asked of Jehovah, and thus I ask of you, the
President of the United States. This is my only pay-
ment, — that which I have received of the Lord, — *aloha,*
(love.) May the love of the Lord Jesus abound with you
until the end of this terrible war in your land."

Alas, that the great and good man to whom it was addressed, did not live to see this letter ! When it reached
Washington our whole land was in mourning.

CHAPTER XVII.

HER LAST VISIT TO MICRONESIA.

ON the 17th of July, 1865, we went on board the *Morning Star* at Honolulu, not to return to the Gilbert Islands, as we longed to do, but to bid " good-bye " to our fellow-laborers who were to sail for Micronesia.   Among them was Mr. Snow, who had so kindly left his work at Ebon to assist in caring for me on the passage to Honolulu.   It was hard to part with your dear little vessel !

Rev. Mr. Emerson of Waialua, who sailed in her, and touched at all the stations in Micronesia, has given an account of what he saw.   He first visited Tarawa, where there were two Hawaiian missionaries, Mahoe and Haina, of whom he speaks as follows : " These brethren have been about five years in this field. . . . They have erected two good-sized meeting-houses and two school-houses. . . . Their own buildings were mainly erected by their own hands, and all look neat and more comfortable than we at first enjoyed at the Sandwich Islands. . . . I could not but admire these laborers, as men and women of warm hearts and true devotion to the cause of our Lord and Master ; and we shall expect to hear that He has honored them in His service."

From Tarawa the *Morning Star* went to Apaiang.   I am very thankful to learn with how much interest the people heard from Mr. Snow an account of my sickness and return to this country, and to know that the king and queen continued to " run well."   While Mr. Emerson saw less evidence of the Spirit's presence among the Gilbert Islanders than elsewhere, still he says, " There is much occasion to give thanks and take courage."

The prayer-meeting which Mr. Emerson attended the Wednesday evening he spent at Ebon, " was one of peculiar interest, and showed that there was a Christian feeling among a people so recently heathen. Although but partially clothed, their appearance was every way becoming and decent." At an examination of the schools there were present one hundred and twenty-five pupils, of whom forty-four could repeat the Gospel of Mark. (How many in the United States can do this ?)

At Kusaie the Lord's work was advancing in a very remarkable manner. They had only a part of the New Testament; but they were studying it very carefully, Mr. Emerson says, " Not to know *whether* things are so, for of that they have no doubt, but to know *what* they are. The Gospel of John, which they have had for a year or more, is committed entirely to memory by many. That this people have simple, child-like confidence in God, is so apparent that no one can mistake it."

Leaving Mr. Snow with his people on Kusaie, the *Morning Star* went on to Ponape, where Mr. and Mrs. Sturges had been for four years alone, with more than they could do, earnestly begging for some one to come and help them. They were, therefore, very glad to see Mr. and Mrs. Doane, who were to be their fellow-laborers. Mr. Emerson spent two weeks on this island, visiting different places, and finding much to interest him in the progress of the Gospel.

Two new stations were commenced during this voyage. Kanoa and Maka were placed on Butaritari, (leaving Aumai and Kapu in charge of Apaiang,) and Kapali was transferred from Namerik to Jaluit, (leaving Kaelemakule alone.) On the former of these it was difficult to gain a foothold ; but " after much talk " the king consented to receive the two Hawaiians. Mr. Snow felt that it was well Kanoa was present; for it needed " all his amiable skill " to succeed. The people feared that if the missionaries came, they would be obliged to give up all their wives but one, and that all the children would be obliged to attend schools, &c. But Mr. Snow satisfied them that no compulsion would be used.

On the 12th of December, 1865, the *Morning Star* returned to Honolulu, thus ending her voyages as a missionary vessel. She has done a noble work, and honored be her memory! Listen to the testimony of Rev. Mr. Damon, Seamen's Chaplain at Honolulu, and editor of the " Friend ": " Having advocated the building of the *Morning Star*, having been present on her arrival at Honolulu in 1857, having witnessed her frequent departures for Micronesia and Marquesas, having welcomed her arrival from those distant missionary fields, having once made a delightful voyage in her through the Micronesian Islands, and having been fully conversant with the management of the little craft, during the entire period that she has been sailing in the service of missions, it affords me much pleasure in bearing testimony to the great assistance which she has rendered the missionary cause. A great and good work has been accomplished by her aid. The hundred thousand stockholders could not have invested their ' dimes ' in a more paying enterprise."

CHAPTER XVIII.

CONCLUSION.

I HAVE now told my story. But before we bid adieu to our little vessel, let us take a parting glance at the work which the *Morning Star* has helped the missionaries, American and Hawaiian, to do. Of their labors in reducing four languages to writing, in translating portions of the Scriptures into as many tongues, and in preparing good books in the same, I cannot speak at length.

We have seen that when the *Morning Star* first visited Micronesia not a single convert had been baptized. Only a few pages had been printed, and that in a single language. Now two Gospels have been printed in the Marshall Island and Kusaiean languages, one quarter of the

New Testament in the Gilbert Island language, more
than one Gospel in the Ponapean, to say nothing of hymn-
books, primers, and other books in all the four languages.

Go with me to Ponape, and let Mr. Sturges point you
to more than two thousand persons, who "are now by
choice and in their sympathies on the Lord's side."
"There is much light on our little island," he says.
"Everywhere the people are eager to hear the truth.
One entire tribe has abandoned heathenism and declared
itself ' missionary.' " Places and objects, once held sacred,
are now treated with scorn. " The highest priests tell
me, and tell the crowd, that their gods and their teach-
ings were all false. Every available reader is put to
work in teaching ' the book ; ' and it is very gratifying to
see the progress many are making." He can point you
to large congregations, " clothed and in their right mind."
He can show you his churches with nearly two hundred
church-members, whom he believes to be true Christians.

And now Mr. Snow will wish you to visit Kusaie, that
you may see the people whom he left nearly four years ago.
He can show you a Sabbath-school of one hundred and
eighteen pupils, of all ages, sitting in little circles on the
floor. some of the classes touching the backs of others, and
yet with no disturbance or confusion. He can point you
to groups of Christians hungry for the Word of Life, lying
around their little jacket-lamps at night, working their
way through the new Gospel of Matthew or the new hymn-
book, just taken out to them in the *Morning Star*. He
will tell you that he never made a tour of the island when
he found so much to cheer his heart. Of the people he
will bear this striking testimony : " Formerly stupid as
death, indifferent as the grave, they are now intensely interested in the Word and the Work of Life."

And you must go to Ebon also, and see the little
church gathered among those wild savages, to whom the
Morning Star took Dr. Pierson and Mr. Doane in 1857.
When once on the Marshall Islands, however, you may
be sure that the Hawaiian missionaries will hold you fast,

till you shall have looked in upon their congregations and
their schools. But you will be richly repaid for the delay,
when you hear Aea (who is supported by the children
of American missionaries at the Sandwich Islands) asking you, as he does his patrons, to praise God with him
by singing a Hawaiian hymn, (227 or 161,) on account
of his converts, beloved of Christ, who are valiant soldiers
of the cross. He will say of them, " They are very bold
in their work. If they meet a person in the road or
elsewhere, they stop him and propose to hold a meeting.
. . . They exhort their chiefs, having no fear of men, but
remembering Him who is able to destroy the soul in hell."

I could wish to show you some fruit on the Gilbert
Islands, but I have said enough. The good work is still
going forward. The harvest is ripening, and soon, we
trust, these isles of Micronesia will be full of the praise
of our Saviour King, to whom be all the glory !

And now, my dear young friends, I must bid you
"farewell" Very pleasant has it been for me to do what
I have done, in telling you the story of your vessel. I
love the Morning Star, my home for so many months upon
the deep, when about my Master's business. Many a
thrill has she sent through my heart. By the blessing of
God she has saved my life. Why should I not love her,
and her owners too ? Why should I not, with a full
heart, tell them of her, — of the good she has done to
me, to my companions, and to the dying heathen ? How
could I consent to part with her, except in the confident
hope that soon another and better "children's vessel "
would be ready to bear me hence again,

"Far in heathen lands to dwell,"

her sails filled with the breath of prayer from ten times
ten thousand youthful hearts ! Gentle reader, farewell !

> "And when our labors all are o'er,
> Then we shall meet to part no more, —
> Meet with the blood-bought throng, to fall,
> And crown our Jesus, Lord of all !"

APPENDIX.

SPECIMENS OF MICRONESIAN LANGUAGES.

THE LORD'S PRAYER IN THE GILBERT ISLAND LANGUAGE.

Tamara are i karawa, e na tabuaki aram.　E na roko ueam: E na tauaki am taeka i aon te aba n ai aron tauana i karawa.　Ko na ananira karara ae ti a tau iai n te bon aei.　Ao ko na kabara ara buakaka mairoura n ai arora nkai ti kabara te buakaka mairouia akana ioawa nako ira.　Ao tai kairira nakon te kaririaki, ma ko na kamaiuira man te buakaka; ba ambai te uea, ao te maka, ao te neboaki, n aki toki.　Amene.

THE LORD'S PRAYER IN THE MARSHALL ISLAND LANGUAGE.

Jememuij i lon, en kwojarjar etom.　En itok am ailin.　Jen komonmen ankil am i kd enwot dri lon.　Ranin, letok son kim kijim ranin: Im jokok amuij jerawiwi, enwot kimuij jokok an armij jerawiwi jen kim.　Im jab tellok son mon, ak drebij kim jen nana.　Bwe am ailin, im kajur, im wijtak in drio.　Amen.

THE LORD'S PRAYER IN THE KUSAIEAN LANGUAGE.

Papa tumus su in kosao, Elos oal payi.　Togusai lalos tuku.　Orek ma nu fwalu, ou elos oru in kosao.　Kite kit len si iwi ma kut mono misini: A nunok munas nu ses ke ma koluk las, oanu kut nanok munas sin met orek ma koluk nu ses.　A tiu kol kia kut in mel, a es kit la liki ma koluk, tu togusai lalos, a ku, a mwolanu, ma patpat.　Amen.

FIRST VERSE OF "THERE IS A HAPPY LAND," IN THE PONAPEAN LANGUAGE.

"Uaja kajulelia.
Meto, meto,
Uaja en aai man,
Marain, marain:
Ar kaul mekajaleL
Jijuj koau kamauri kit,
Kitail kaul laut er kaul,
Kaul maraare."

Printed in the USA
CPSIA information can be obtained
at www.ICGtesting.com
LVHW011504061023
760358LV00003B/25

9 781016 678824